For all those who love to draw,
especially those who don't know it yet.

ACKNOWLEDGMENTS

Thank you to my family and friends for their continued support and encouragement! A big whale-sized thank you to my wife, Thasja, for her support, ever-helpful feedback, and patience with me during this latest creative journey. And once again, my heartfelt appreciation to the entire Design Studio Press family for their assistance, guidance, and enthusiasm. Thank you to Des & Kerry Hegarty for 'The Amazing Mr A!' ('U-umph' to Tilly). And finally, a large dose of gratitude to all the authors and illustrators who inspired me to draw at an early age. I'd be tickled if this book could achieve something similar for today's budding artists.

To contact the artist please visit
WWW.CHRISAYERSDESIGN.COM

Published by Design Studio Press
8577 Higuera Street
Culver City, CA 90232
http://www.designstudiopress.com
E-mail: info@designstudiopress.com
10 9 8 7 6 5 4 3 2 1

Printed in China
First Edition, May 2011

ISBN 13: 978-1933492163-6

Library of Congress Control Number: 2011925059

my the daily zoo

a drawing activity book for all ages

this book is a
collaboration of imagination
between CHRIS AYERS and

_____

(your name here!)

designstudio|PRESS

THE STORY OF THE DAILY ZOO

I started the DAILY ZOO a year after being diagnosed with acute myelogenous leukemia, a type of blood cancer. Undergoing the physical and emotional stresses of treatment and recovery was a tumultuous journey and reminded me just how unpredictable life can be.

After surviving the cancer roller coaster, which left me both figuratively and literally nauseous, I wanted to make sure I celebrated the GIFT OF EACH HEALTHY DAY. To help me achieve this it made sense to enlist the help of two of my lifelong passions: animals and drawing. My goal was to draw one animal each day for a year.

Though challenging at times, I accomplished my goal. I drew an animal each day for a year...and beyond. (At the time of this writing I am wrapping up Year Five—1800 days and counting!) It has proven to be a very therapeutic endeavor and I have been fortunate to have had the opportunity to publish the first two years' worth of sketches in The Daily Zoo: Keeping the Doctor at Bay with a Drawing a Day and The Daily Zoo Year Two.

One of the effects I hope the Daily Zoo books have on readers is to inspire them to exercise and explore their own creativity, ideally on a daily basis. In fact, Des Hegarty, a talented and passionate school teacher in England, discovered the books and added his own creativity to the mix by penning 'The Amazing Mr A!' (which you can read on the following pages) as another way of encouraging his students to create.

Make pursuing your passions a HABIT! It matters not what "medium" you choose—it could be art, singing, cooking, mathematics, science (the possibilities are endless!)—it just matters that you do what you love to do. It will ENRICH YOUR LIFE.

Which leads us to this book: MY Daily Zoo. I wanted to provide people, especially children, with an opportunity to get creative and use their imaginations. Creativity is empowering. Developing creative problem-solving skills at an early age can lead to a lifetime of innovation and thinking outside the box. With this book, I've provided some tips and nudges, but it's up to YOU and YOUR IMAGINATION to really make the experience complete.

So without further ado, let's sharpen those pencils and START DRAWING!!!

THE AMAZING MR A!

(or How a Drawing a Day Keeps the Sadness Away)

by Des Hegarty,
teacher at Wilbury Primary in England, and
his lovely wife, Kerry

This story tells, in an extraordinary way,
The incredible journey of 'The Amazing Mr A!'
An imaginative artist who, surprised to say
Began to feel ill on one very odd day.

So Dr Bob and Nurse Jen were called and they said,
"Mr A you are sick and you must stay in bed.
Your condition is serious, and what we suggest
Is medicine, love and plenty of rest."
Advice followed on, from the good Doctor and Nurse,
That before he got better, Mr A would feel worse.

Mr A was stunned and didn't know what to say
And for the first time ever his "Amazing" went away.
His smile had reversed and drooped upside down.
He couldn't think of how to turn it around.
All were concerned that such a dazzling young man
Should be so melancholy—thus treatment began!

Then it happened one very special, magic day,
As the once "Amazing" Mr A lay
He heard a voice and this voice did say,
"Pick up a pencil and don't delay!"

The bulb above his head was brilliantly bright
And an idea exploded, like creative dynamite!
"I will sketch what I love, I know what to do!"
And he started drawing animals for "The Daily Zoo."
This is where his adventure really began
His 'amazing' talent poured out - as only talent can!

He drew ...
Sharks at the opera,
A crow looking mean,
A sad clown hyena,
A tree frog that's green,
An embarrassed rabbit
And a waiting room bear,
A newt to the rescue,
But he didn't stop there!

He drew ...
Sea dragon Lenny
And a cool cockatoo,
Giraffes eye to eye
And a left-handed ewe,
A furry tree dweller
And Dung Beetle Don,
A frog with huge eyebrows,
The list just goes on!

He drew...
A tiger burning bright,
And a speeding cheetah.
A blue-footed booby
And a hippo called Rita!
Constable Komodo
Flamingo Fu!
Undunts and elephants
And a kicking kangaroo!

He drew ...
Penguins on stilts
And a hunched chimpanzee,
A rhino, an afghan
And a dog-eating tree!
A very tired tortoise,
A bulldog at war,
(I'll think I'll stop now,
But I know there are more!)

He shared these pictures so all could look,
And put them together in a marvelous book.
Copies were bound and reached far and wide.
His animals enthralled and made you chuckle inside!
(Ha-Ha-Ha!)

Every single animal creation
Added to his eventual rehabilitation
(He was getting better folks!)
And gradually his "Amazing" returned.
He saw life again, and what he had learned
Was that a drawing a day,
Keeps the sadness away.

So pick up your pencil—don't delay!
Pick up a pencil - join 'The Amazing Mr A!'
Do what you love and love what you do.
Enjoy drawing pictures with 'The Daily Zoo!'

START SIMPLE!

Drawing doesn't have to be intimidating. If you can draw basic shapes such as this circle, square, and triangle, then with practice and observation you can use them as building blocks to draw just about anything!

  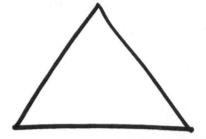

ALL OF US HERE AT THE DAILY ZOO, NO MATTER HOW COMPLEX OR SIMPLE WE ARE, CAN BE BROKEN DOWN INTO BASIC SHAPES.

HEY! WHO YOU CALLIN' "SIMPLE?"

By changing the shape, size and proportions of these building blocks we can create an endless variety of characters. I used the simple drawings at right to make three apes. They are all gorillas, but because they are built using different combinations of shapes, they become three unique characters.

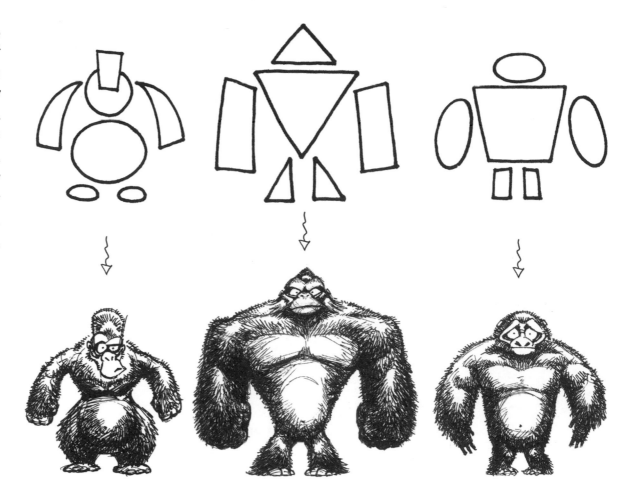

Now it's your turn! Start by creating a very simple character using rectangles, triangles, and circles. Then start to add details like eyes, a mouth, and things like fingers and toes.

DRAW IT HERE! ⟿

ANIMAL ALPHABET

Design your own alphabet characters and then use them to introduce yourself to Nuke on the opposite page!

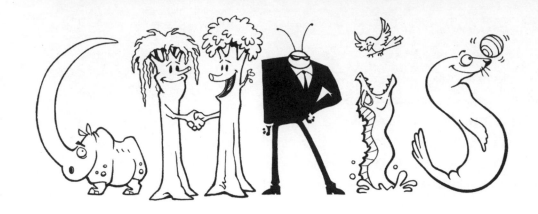

 B C D

I J K L M

R S T U V

My name is _____

E F G H

N O P Q

W X Y Z

WHAT MAKES A FROG A FROG?

When drawing animals it helps to know what animals look like! Go to zoos and aquariums and farms and dog parks. Look at pictures of animals in books, magazines, and the Internet. Watch programs about animals on television. Get to know them and draw what you see!

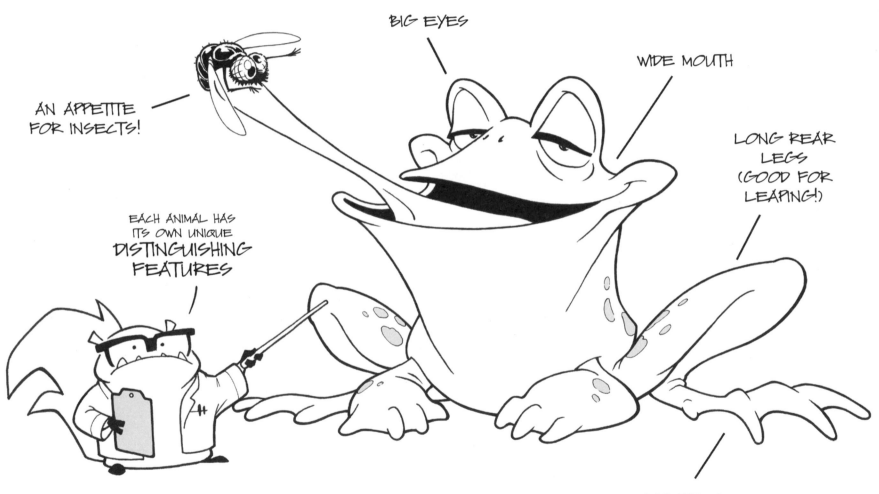

BIG EYES

WIDE MOUTH

AN APPETITE FOR INSECTS!

LONG REAR LEGS (GOOD FOR LEAPING!)

EACH ANIMAL HAS ITS OWN UNIQUE DISTINGUISHING FEATURES

LONG TOES (OFTEN WEBBED)

Because individual species of a certain type of animal can vary, there are of course exceptions to these rules. We can also take some artistic license, especially when drawing cartoon animals, but knowing these general features at least gives us a starting point.

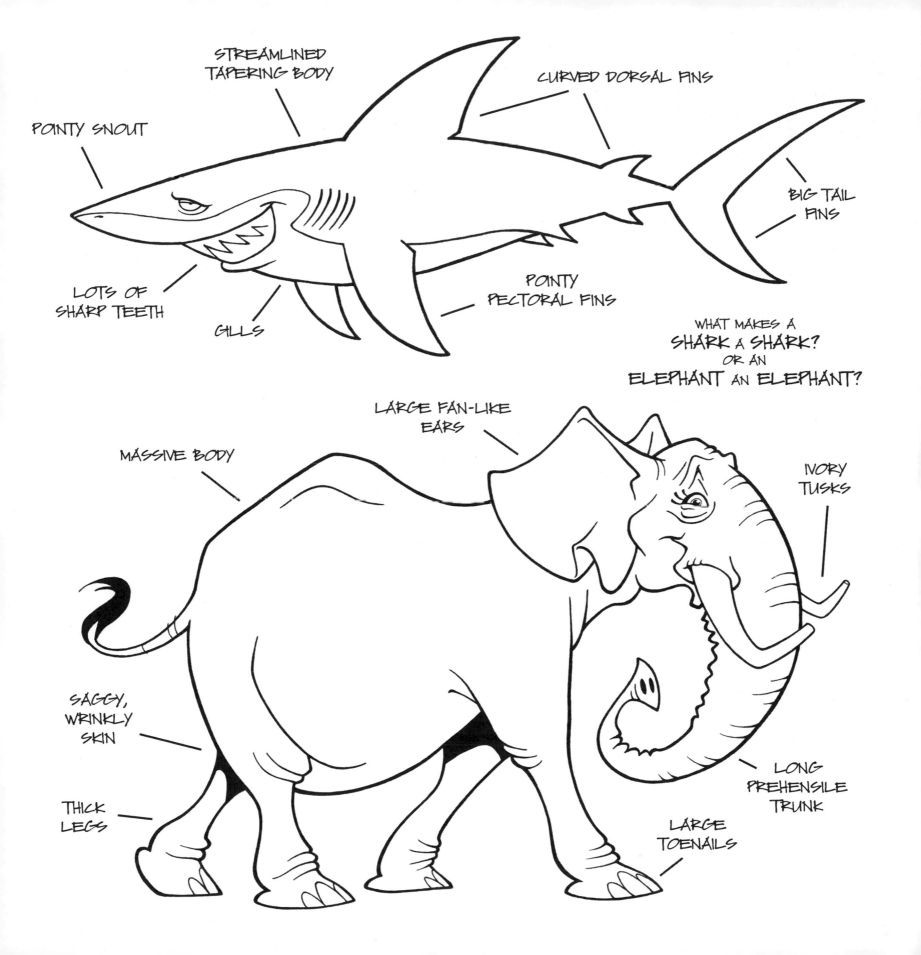

LET'S GET SQUIGGLY!

Before we go any further, let's warm up our imagination and drawing hands by doing some squiggle exercises.

1. Make a squiggle.

2. Let your imagination go wild and try to "see" a character in the squiggle. What do you see? A face? A mouth? A tail? Legs? Wings? Ears?

3. Draw that character!

Squiggle + imagination = character!

Now make some of your own squiggles and squiggle friends!

DON'T BE AFRAID TO TURN THE PAGE—OR YOURSELF—UPSIDE DOWN TO GET ANOTHER LOOK. YOU MIGHT SEE SOMETHING COMPLETELY DIFFERENT!

Nuke the Squirrel

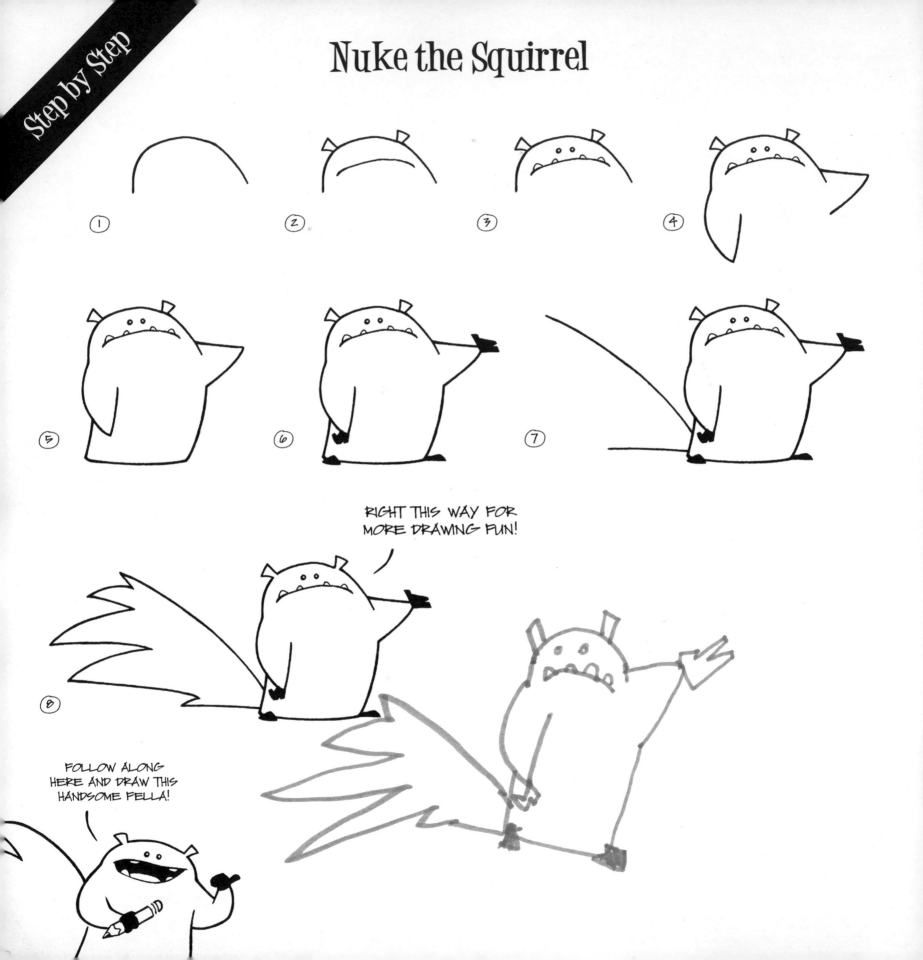

RIGHT THIS WAY FOR MORE DRAWING FUN!

FOLLOW ALONG HERE AND DRAW THIS HANDSOME FELLA!

Polychromatic Hippos day 114

Polychromatic means "many colors" but since this book is printed in black and white it's up to YOU to give them the funky colors they deserve.

Most hippos like to dance, but polychromatic hippos don't just dance...they BOOGIE!

Orson the Owl

①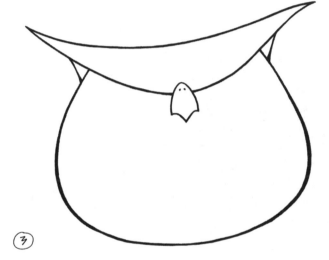

②

③

④

⑤

⑥

⑦

⑧

⑨

⑩

DON'T WORRY IF YOUR OWL LOOKS DIFFERENT THAN ORSON HERE. THAT'S OK BECAUSE HE'S YOUR OWL!

COMPLETE-A-CRITTER

Fill in these beastly blanks!

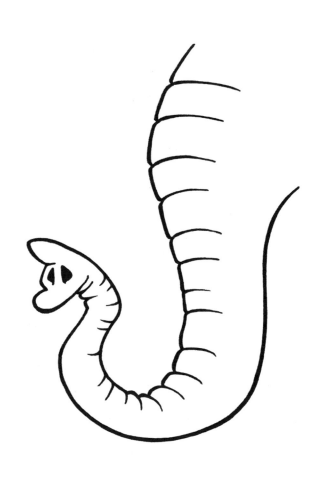

Toola Turtle

1

2

3

4

5

6

⑦

⑧

⑨

⑩

Mac the Octopus
day 1634

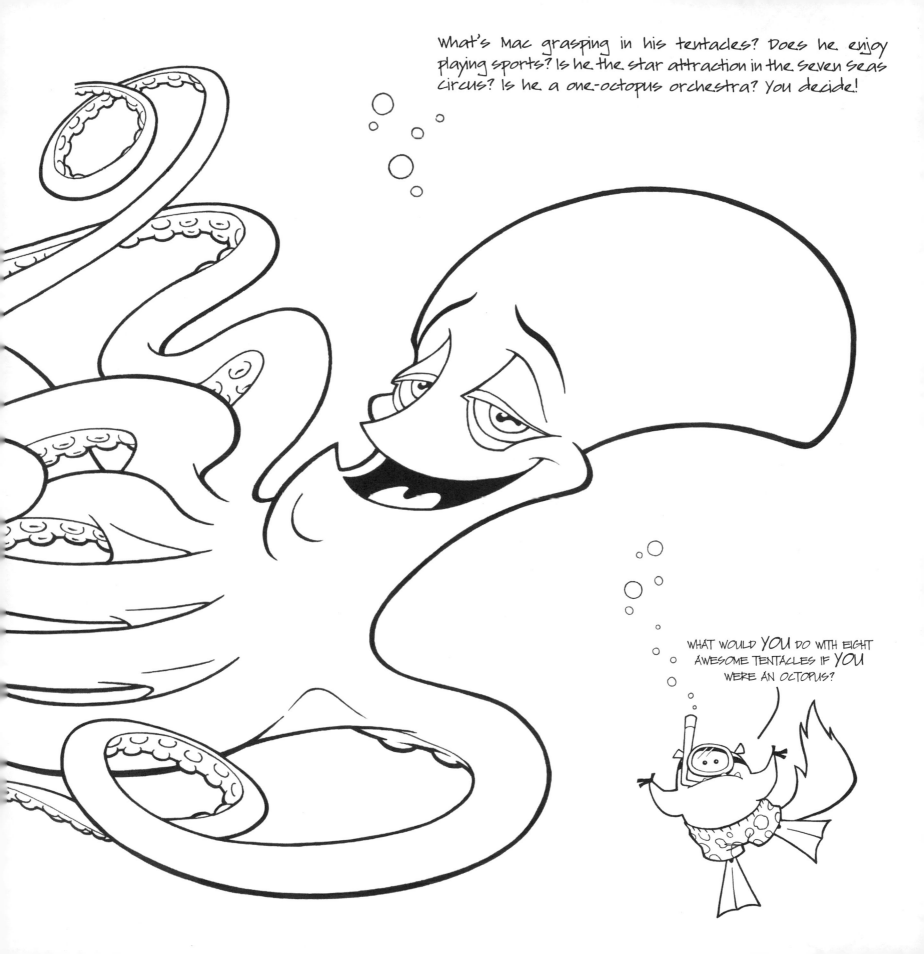

What's Mac grasping in his tentacles? Does he enjoy playing sports? Is he the star attraction in the Seven Seas Circus? Is he a one-octopus orchestra? You decide!

WHAT WOULD YOU DO WITH EIGHT AWESOME TENTACLES IF YOU WERE AN OCTOPUS?

Sammy Sardine

① ② ③

④ ⑤ ⑥

⑦ ⑧ ⑨

⑩

FOLLOW
ALONG
HERE!

Gordy Grouper

1
2
3
4
5
6
7
8
9
10

CATCH OF THE DAY

Who caught what?

Did you know?
GRIZZLY BEARS ARE EXCELLENT
AT CATCHING FISH. MOST DON'T
EVEN USE POLES!

Selena Sea Horse

① ② ③ ④

⑤ ⑥

⑦ ⑧

Cornelius Crab

1

2

3

4

5

6

7

8

UNDER THE SEA

This coral reef needs some fish!

SWITCH IT UP!

Normally I draw with my right hand, but sometimes I like to switch it up and draw left-handed. I'm not as practiced when I do this so my drawings can be more unpredictable and lead me to discover new shapes and ideas in the "mistakes."

Right hand →

← Left hand

Draw something with your left paw!

Draw something with your right paw!

Did you know?
WHEN GIVEN THE OPPORTUNITY SOME ANIMALS IN CAPTIVITY, SUCH AS ELEPHANTS, PRIMATES, AND DOLPHINS, HAVE SHOWN GREAT SKILL AND INTEREST IN PAINTING.

Pepe the Mischievous Monkey

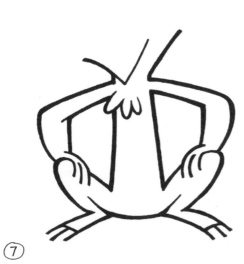

10

11

12

Where are all the other jungle creatures?

All these eyes see you, but who do YU see?

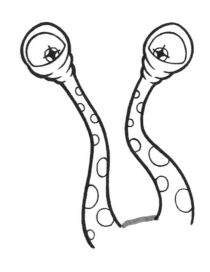

Babirusa *day 498*

Bamboo Bob looks pretty frightened.
What's he running from?

NAME: Artie Amore

HEIGHT: 4' 7"   WEIGHT: 182 lbs.

SPECIES: American Alligator

EYES: Yellow   HAIR: N/A

FUR ☐ FEATHERS ☐ SCALES ☒

HOMETOWN: Baton Rouge, LA

OCCUPATION: Toothbrush Salesgator

FAVORITE FOOD: Anchovy sundaes

LIKES: FISHING, KARAOKE TUESDAYS, GOOD ORAL HYGIENE HABITS, TOOTHPICKS, FLOSS, MAKING A SALE, SPICY FOODS, SINGING IN THE SHOWER (ESPECIALLY SINATRA TUNES)

DISLIKES: SLOW DRIVERS, SUB-FREEZING TEMPERATURES, DIRT, BASIC CABLE, CAVITIES, LEATHER GOODS

FAVORITE VACATION DESTINATION: EVERGLADES NATIONAL PARK

LAST BOOK READ: USER'S MANUAL FOR THE POWERSCRUB 3000 ELECTRIC TOOTHBRUSH

NAME: Purple Patattie

HEIGHT: 2'7"   WEIGHT: unknown

SPECIES: unknown

EYES: Purple   HAIR: Purple Frizz

FUR ☑ FEATHERS ☑ SCALES ☐

HOMETOWN: unknown

OCCUPATION: unknown

FAVORITE FOOD: anything Purple

LIKES: Purple, itself, and burping, hair.

DISLIKES: Farting, Parties,

FAVORITE VACATION DESTINATION: unknown

LAST BOOK READ: none (it does not read)

LAUGHS THE HARDEST WHEN: Someone says butt

FAVORITE SCHOOL SUBJECT: none

Sticky
Predicament
day 424

WHAT'S GOING THROUGH ROSCOE'S HEAD? HOW HE GOT INTO THIS MESS—OR HOW HE'S GOING TO GET OUT OF IT?

Brutus the Bulldog

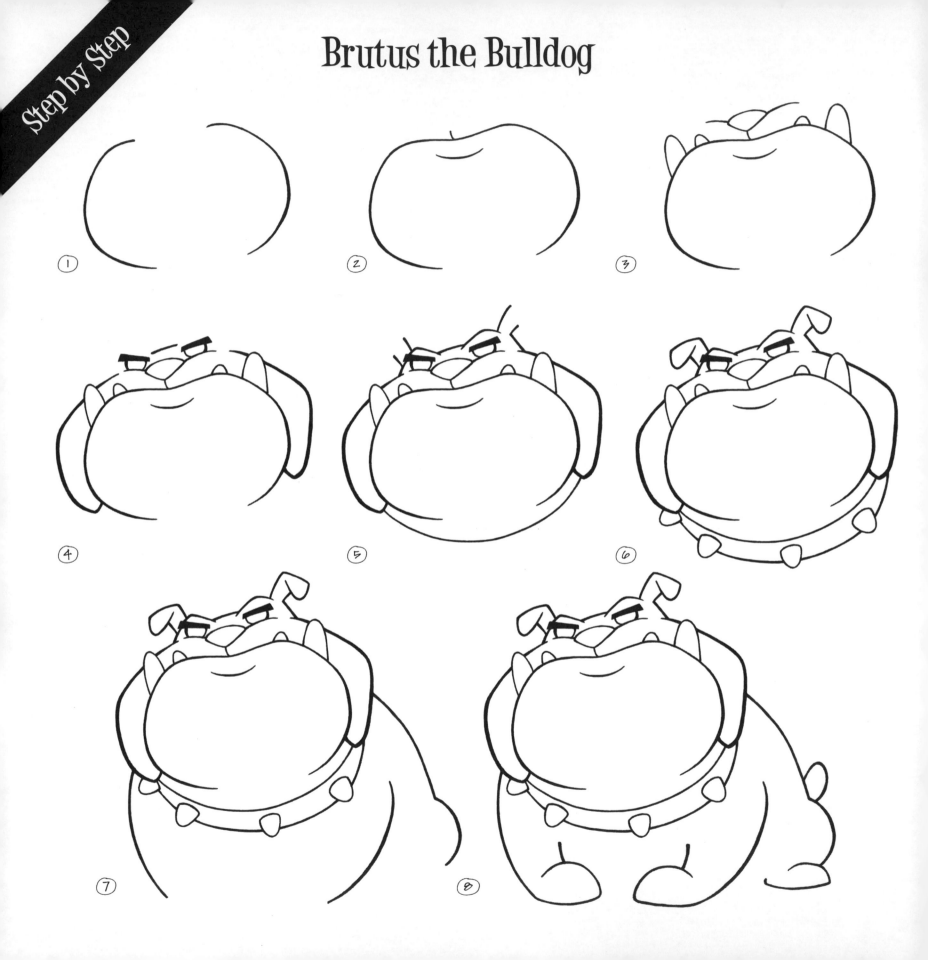

9

10

Al E. Cat

①

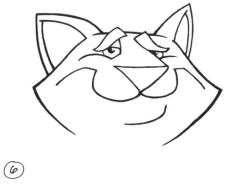

②

③

④

⑤

⑥

⑦

⑧

⑨

10

11

Abracadab-wha?!!
day 1793

What has
MAX the
MAGNIFICENT
pulled from his
magical hat?

THE DREAM PET

If you could have any animal in the world—this world or any other—for a pet, what would it be? Would it wear a collar? Would it live in a cage? An aquarium? Under your bed?

Would you take it for a walk? A swim? A hop? A slither? What would you feed it? How big or small is it? Don't forget to give it a name!

Ebo the Elephant

1

2

3

4

5

6

7

8

⑨

⑩

The Tusk Fairy

day 589

When Matron Matilda is not moonlighting as the Tusk Fairy, she teaches at the Fleewick Academy for Fairies. Can you draw her flighty students?

Droop-billed
Snipe
day 707

Party in Pink

Add yourself or your favorite animal
to the conga line!

Not of a Feather
day 488

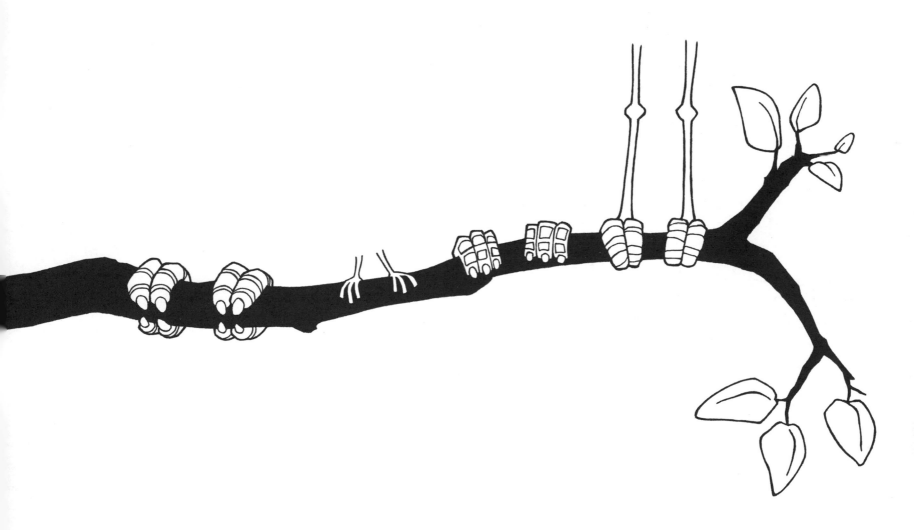

Birds come in all shapes, sizes, colors, & patterns.
Create some of your own feathered friends!

The Brainstorm Bag!

On the days when I'm stuck for an idea for the Daily Zoo, I will often turn to my trusty Brainstorm Bag, filled with lots of paper scraps. On each piece I've written the name of an animal...or a noun, verb, adjective, or adverb. I reach in and grab a few pieces and then try to make a drawing using those words, like this gopher cowboy.

Licorice Lassoin' Gopher
day 306

"GOPHER" + "LICORICE" = Why, a cowboy rodent dancing with his licorice lasso, of course!

TRY THIS!

Choose a few words from the lists at right and combine them to create a character. For example, what would a SMELLY TURTLE PIRATE be EATING? Or what would be making the GIRAFFE OPERA SINGER SAD?

lion	reading	broom	doctor	smelly
giraffe	eating	camera	pirate	sad
fox	flying	ice cream	opera singer	noisy
turtle	cleaning	cape	farmer	small

YOU CAN MAKE YOUR OWN BRAINSTORM BAG!

The last page of this book is a Brainstorm Bag starter kit. Carefully tear out the sheet and separate the individual words along the perforations. Stick them in a bag and PRESTO! One Brainstorm Bag at your service!

1. Shake the bag
2. Grab some words
3. Turn on your imagination
4. Start drawing!

Frank, one of the keepers here at the DAILY ZOO, has to make sure all of the animals are healthy. This includes brushing their teeth! What creature is happy to see him today?

UNDER THE BIG TOP
Complete these FANTABULOUS circus acts!

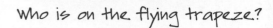

Who is on the flying trapeze?

The Amazing Ugo
day 403

What other objects is this unicycling uakari juggling?

Who is the sword swallower? OUCH!

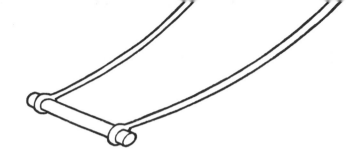

Draw the Ringmaster!

Who's the daredevil cannonballer?

A circus wouldn't be a circus without clowns, right? But one needs a face!

LADIES AND GENTLEMEN, I GIVE YOU THE EVER-POPULAR AND EVER-PRECISE ACROBATIC FEATS OF THE

POSITIVELY PERPLEXING PENGUINIS!!!

(HAVE YOU EVER SEEN ANYTHING SO PREPOSTEROUS?)

Now create your very own
GREATEST SHOW ON EARTH!

Bucking Bronco day 577

Who's getting bucked?

ANIMAL CHOP-SHOP

In addition to drawing real animals, I enjoy using my imagination to make up my own creatures. It can be fun to mix and match parts of different animals to create an entirely new species.

Jackamoose
day 033

Storkoise
day 311

I'M 100% ALL NATURAL, BABY!

Platypus
day 1282

Did you know?
WHEN EARLY EXPLORERS FIRST BROUGHT A STUFFED PLATYPUS SPECIMEN BACK TO ENGLAND, IT WAS THOUGHT TO BE A HOAX BECAUSE IT LOOKED LIKE IT WAS A MISH-MASH OF SEVERAL DIFFERENT ANIMALS.

Mix and match the animal body parts on this page to create your own unique creatures!

PIG   SEAGULL   OWL   SNAKE   ANTEATER

BUTTERFLY

STRIPES? SPOTS?

ELEPHANT

SHARK

MOUSE

RABBIT

HORSE

GRASSHOPPER

SNAIL   SKUNK   CAMEL   OCTOPUS   FROG

Now use the following "recipes" to explore more fantastic creature creation!

PEACOCK ⟿

PEACROCK

⟿ CROCODILE

RING-TAILED LEMUR ⟿
& FROG

RING-TAILED FROG

⟿ GIANT PANDA

KANGAROO ⟿⟶

KANGAPOTAMUS

⟵⟿ HIPPOPOTAMUS

MUSK OX ⟿⟶

_____

⟵⟿ YOUR CHOICE!

What just hatched?

Rhinoceros Ralph

① ② ③ ④

⑤ ⑥

⑦ ⑧

9

10

11

Eye to Eye *day 302*

You and I are basically the same.
Though we may each answer to a different name.
No reason we can't see eye to eye
If all we do is simply try.

Who else is seeing eye to eye?

Waiting Room Bear day 348

On this day I spotted a big bear of a man while waiting to see my doctor, so I drew him as an actual bear!

Draw your friends or family as animal characters!

If you could be any animal, which would you be?

So many choices! From land, air, and sea!

Just one more drawing before we bid adieu,

So look in the mirror and draw the ANIMAL YOU!

KEEP ON
DRAWING!!! !!!!

astronaut	water-skiing	bow tie	striped	elephant
mad scientist	ballroom dancing	treasure chest	frightened	shark
super hero	cooking	guitar	lucky	owl
king/queen	juggling	balloon	charming	alligator
lumberjack	swimming	sunglasses	grumpy	platypus
rock star	bowling	jetpack	surprised	dragon
clown	dreaming	polka dots	sleepy	hippo
secret agent	hanging	mud	happy	penguin
wizard	skateboarding	tuba	strong	monkey
couch potato	playing soccer	pizza	sneaky	frog